A Season for Emmaline
November 2000

To Everything there is a season, and a time to every purpose under the heaven:

A time to be born and a time to die;
a time to plant and a time to pluck that which is planted;
A time to love and a time to hate;
a time of war, and a time of peace.

He hath made everything beautiful in his time...

ECCLESIASTES chapter 3

MOSAICS

Mosaics, by definition, are pictures or designs made by inlaying small bits of colored stone into mortar.

Beginning centuries ago, mosaics were used to decorate floors and walls. Some of the first known mosaics were basically monochromatic designs made with cockshells, onyx, and clay.

Mosaics, in their medieval form, served a purpose. The textural designs delighted and entertained the eye while sometimes serving as a record of ancient tales.

In the current century, we are surrounded by colorful materials made by man, as well as those found in nature. Recently, the mosaic materials list has been extended to include more personal items such as photographs.

We can continue the mosaic tradition of recording tales by preserving our own stories using photos and paper in a mosaic style.

TOOLS

Things that look complex or difficult are often easier than they seem when you have the right tools.

Mosaic Moments™ Mat - I am frequently asked what makes the Mosaic Moments™ Mat special. When choosing a mat for the photo mosaic process, the biggest consideration is grid size. The Mosaic Moments™ mat has an eighth inch grid system with enhanced marks at half inch and one inch intervals. This allows flexibility during the mosaic process.

In the example to the right, I used a photo of a child standing on a bench. I wanted to maintain the ends of the bench and keep the child's head centered in one square. To do this I had to crop out sections of the photo on each side

of the child. Those sections are not missed in the mosaic. Without my eighth inch grid to help me, eliminating those parts would have been difficult.

Metal Ruler with Cork Backing - Any metal straight edge can be used. A cork backing is preferable to help keep the ruler from slipping out of place while cutting.

Craft Knife, with no.11 blade - When choosing a craft knife, be sure it has a standard no.11 blade.

Do not use a box cutter with a retractable blade or a swiveling craft knife. They will not give you a clean straight cut.

Repositionable Transfer (dots) adhesive - There are many brands of transfer adhesive available in convenient dispensers. Not all of them are repositionable. Be sure to check the packaging.

Photo cloth - Very important for rubbing finger prints off photographs.

Cutting this photo into four even squares was not a good option since one of the cuts would have been through the child's head.

Strips of the photo were eliminated to keep the child's head and the ends of the bench intact.

Step By Step

1. choose 6-10 photographs

Do not pre-crop photographs! It is not necessary to precrop your photos since the mosaic process is a cropping process. You might need "that little bit" of your picture to help with spacing.

Lighting - When choosing pictures for your photo mosaic it is best to look for photographs with similar lighting. Outdoor photos work well.

Subject - Many photographic subjects are enhanced by the Mosaic Process. Scenic outdoor photographs work especially well. Photo mosaics can bring to life photos of activities such as baseball games, Easter Egg hunts, snowman building, or choosing the perfect pumpkin.

People - Photographs with just a couple of people are easiest to work with when cutting photos into one inch squares. I prefer to use photographs where the subject's heads are one inch or smaller in size on the photograph to keep the entire head in one cut square.

Close-ups - Keep in mind that photographs will be cut into smaller pieces. Close up shots may not work well when cut into one inch squares. You may want to consider those photographs for focal points within your mosaic (see examples pages 18 - 19).

Six photos were used to make the above mosaic. Notice how the pathway and large fountain were cut and placed to emphasize their common curves. The photograph of the plant was rearranged to fill an empty space.

Distant shots were placed at the top of the mosaic (in the background) while close up shots were placed toward the bottom of the page (in the foreground.) This gives the mosaic a feeling of spatial perspective - almost as if it had all come from one big picture.

Tip: save all 1x1 inch photo pieces until your mosaic is complete. You never know when you might need a few extra pieces.

Step By Step

2. Cut photographs into one inch squares.

A. Using the 1/8 inch grid as a guide, place photo on mat.

TIP: Put a repositionable transfer adhesive on the back of your photo before you place it on the mat. Be sure to get adhesive on each square inch. Four lines running horizontally across the back of a 4x6 photograph will do the trick.

The repositionable transfer adhesive will keep your photo in position while you are cutting and help you make clean straight cuts.

Determine where to make your first cut.

You may want to leave something intact in your photograph - such as a person's head. Before you cut, determine the focal point of the photo. Begin cutting in a place that will leave important aspects of your focal point uninterrupted. Cut remainder of photograph in one inch increments from that point.

* Do not cut horizontally through a person's eyes or through their chin where this can be avoided.

Cut Photographs -
Cut entire photograph into one inch squares using a craft knife with a no.11 blade and a metal ruler with cork backing.

Additional Tips:

Be sure your craft knife blade is sharp. Dull blades make cutting more difficult.

Cork backing on a ruler helps prevent slipping.

Step By Step
3. Transfer to Mosaic Moments™ Grid Paper.

When you lift your photo pieces off of the mat, they will still have the repositionable adhesive on them. You can now transfer the photo pieces from your mat directly to your grid paper. It's that simple!

If you change your mind about placement, you can easily lift and reposition the photo squares, because the transfer adhesive is repositionable.

As you transfer your photo pieces, check each of them for enough adhesive to keep them securely in place. If coverage looks inadequate simply roll on a bit more.

Repositionable adhesive will become permanent in about 72 hours.

Drawing Your Own Grid

Place a sheet of 12x12 cardstock over your Mosaic Moments™ Mat lining it up with the grid lines.

Use a ruler to draw your first line 3/8 inch (three squares down) from the top of your page. Move your ruler down 1 1/8 inch and make your second line. Continue drawing lines in 1 1/8 inch increments until you have drawn 10 lines.

Turn your page 90 degrees and repeat the process - again starting your lines 3/8 inch from the top of the page.

Place your cut photo squares in the upper left corner of your grid to cover drawn lines, as shown on the Mosaic Moments™ Paper. A small portion of the drawn line will be visible once photo squares have been placed. This can be erased if desired.

Tip:
Be sure to use a very light hand when drawing grid lines.

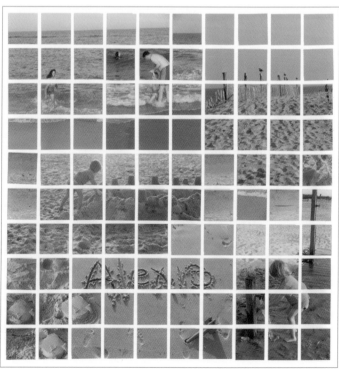

Epcot 2000 -
by Sandi Keene
Williamsburg VA

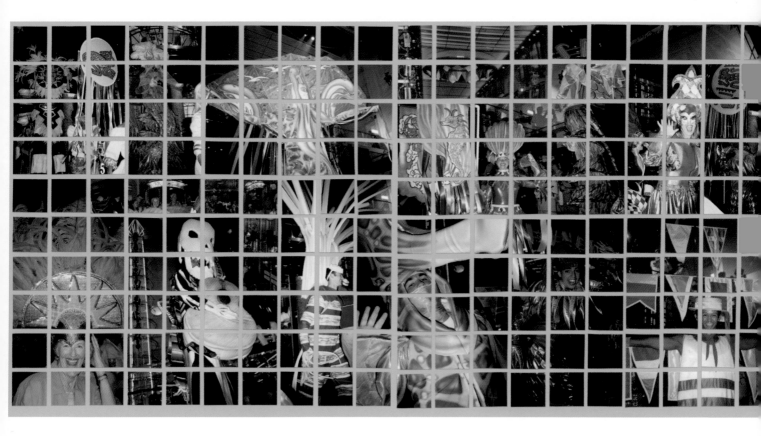

Visual Unity

One of the fun things about Mosaic pages is having the ability to change the view. You can make two people (or more) look like they are in the same photograph - even though they aren't.

It is fun to blend many photographs together to make one big scene. Panoramic style photo mosaics are a great way to show off several related photographs and bring visual unity to the collection.

Above: Mardi Gras Parade
by Joan Hess - *Williamsburg VA*

Right: Catchin' Waves -
by Sandi Keene - *Williamsburg VA*

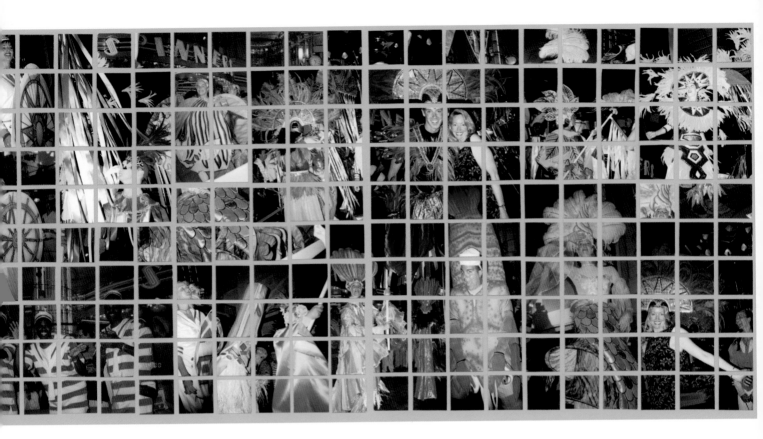

BUILDING BLOCK PAGES

Building blocks come in all sorts of shapes and sizes. The builder can choose to work with all the same size blocks or they can add variety and interest by varying the pattern or the block size.

Working with the Mosaic Moments™ grid paper does not mean you must cut all of your photos into 1x1 inch squares. You can add interest and emphasize focal points by varying the height or width of your photo blocks.

Mosaic Moments™
Quick Grid Guide

2 Squares	2 1/8 inches
3 Squares	3 1/4 inches
4 Squares	4 3/8 inches
5 Squares	5 1/2 inches
6 Squares	6 5/8 inches

The building block process can be easily achieved using your Mosaic Moments™ Mat with eighth inch grid lines.

When using Mosaic Moments™ grid paper, the rule is: add one eighth inch for every additional square. See Mosaic Moments™ quick grid guide.

Simply line up your photographs on the Mosaic Moments™ Mat using the eighth inch guides. Make cuts based on the area you wish to cover.

Treasure Island and Venetian Pages on Mosaic Moments™ squash grid paper

WINGS

Flight To Phoenix
Alexis got her first wings - June 2001

Alexis was so excited to get on the Airplane and make her first trip through the clouds! She especially enjoyed the airplane snacks, sitting next to the window, and her new magic drawing board!

Our American Airlines flight departed on time out of Raleigh NC. We had a layover for about an hour in Dallas Texas before arriving in cactus country -Phoenix Arizona. Our travel group included: Daddy and Mommy (Kevin and Tami) sister, Paije, cousin McKenzie and her husband Derek.

MOSAIC BORDERS

Have you ever taken a picture of a beautiful sunset and then sighed with disappointment when the dramatic vision you remembered came back from the developer?

By using several photographs to build a border you can recapture the essence of the view you remember.

Building a Mosaic border may be the perfect way to use those otherwise uneventful photographs and give your pages new life using your own images.

Above: 4 - 6 cloud photos were used to create the photo mosaic borders. Photos were cut into one inch squares and mounted onto Mosaic Moments™ cloud blue grid paper. The grid paper was trimmed and mounted onto 12x12 white cardstock.

1x1 inch "Stacked cactus" photo blocks were mounted on cardstock cut to show a 1/8 inch border. The blocks filled an awkward gap and added additional information and interest to the layout.

Inside the mosaic image:

We enjoyed our first big snow in Virginia.

hands warm while building a snowman.

Even though we weren't very well prepared

Alexis wore an old pair of socks to keep her

Our First Virginia Snow - January 2000

We have not seen a lot of snow since we moved to the east coast. A light dusting here and there - melted by about 8 AM - seems to be the best we can hope for. This year we experienced a rare treat - enough snow to build a snowman!

Paije was the first one out the door. Alexis was just a step behind her. Not a moment of this fabulous morning would be wasted! Thanks to Paije's creative nature, this snowman got a grill lid for a hat.

SEQUENTIAL MOSAIC PAGES

Making a "time lapse" mosaic page may be the next best thing to watching the event on video! Mosaic pages can be a great way to capture a series of events.

In the page shown above, a focal point was established by mounting a central, un-cut picture in the center of the page. Additional photos were cut into one inch pieces and mounted around the focal point showing the series of

Mirror Mirror on the wall
Who's the most handsome boy of all?

Trey's First Haircut

It was time for Trey's first trim just
one month before his first birthday.
Michelle at the Mirror Mirror Salon did a
great job with our handsome little guy!

July 13, 2000

events that lead up to the "finished product."

Above: 1x1 inch cardstock pieces were used to frame the focal point photo, separating it from the surrounding photographs, to give it further emphasis.

Additional interest is added to this mosaic design by cutting the two photographs on each side of the central photo into 2 1/8 inch squares.

A Season Filled with Festive Fun

Chrysanthemums, scarecrows, and magical mirrors are discovered by Alexis as she enjoys fall through the eyes of a four year old.

Busch Gardens   Williamsburg, Virginia   October 2001

ADDING TITLES

Adding titles to Mosaic Pages offers the opportunity to describe the photographs used. Titles can be treated as borders or included in squares used for Journaling.

Above: Chrysanthemums are a fall favorite and a great subject for photo mosaics. The 2 square x 6 square title was inset allowing the mosaic to wrap completely around it.

Top right: Stickers are added to layered Alphaduets™ giving this full width, border style title a dimensional look with eye catching accents.

Lower Right: Animal Kingdom Page
by Sandi Keene - *Williamsburg VA*

Mosaic Moments™ Quick Title Guide

Height x   (see Quick Grid guide page 15)

Width

12x12 page full width	11 1/8 inches
8.5x11 page full width	7 6/8 inches
6 Squares	6 5/8 inches

Grids Are Great

From checker boards to basket weaving, the creative possibilities are endless! Great results are quickly achieved using Mosaic Moments™ grid paper or your own grid design (see drawing your own grid page 9) as your guide. Simply remember the rules (see Quick Grid Guide page 15) and you are on your way.

Try using various solid or patterned papers in rectangle and square shapes to frame a photo or build a checkered border (see page 28.) Use papers that enhance the theme of your photographs.

Cut photos. Cut paper. Add stickers, journaling blocks, and titles. Whether you have one great photo, or several, designing with grid paper can help fill the gaps, add interest, and give your pages a sense of organization.

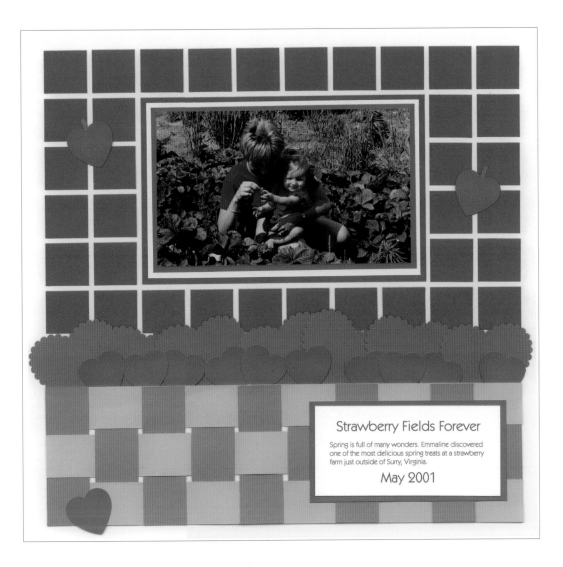

Above L: Simplistic style and festive colors create a frame for this Halloween photograph. A rectangle title block is sized and positioned to reflect the space used for journaling. Balancing these two elements maintains the symmetrical design.

Above: Picking strawberries, a cherished spring event, was recorded in this photograph and given a prominent place on this scrapbook page.

A woven basket look was created using strips of 1 inch x 11 1/8 inch paper woven horizontally through 1 inch x 3 1/4 inch paper strips.

Horizontal paper strips are attached to the grid paper at one end. Shorter strips are then worked into the long strips using an under/overlap system leaving eighth inch gaps between strips.

A row of red hearts is placed in front of a row of green scalloped edge hearts to give the impression of strawberries in a basket.

Greensboro, North Carolina June 2001

Alexis and Ashley Paije spent a lot of time swimming this summer. Paije swam under the water while Alexis learned to blow bubbles in the water. Alexis loves her floating suit - purchased on our trip to Arizona for a Family Reunion day at the lake .

Alexis got good use out of the suit again at the Courtyard hotel pool when we went to Greensboro, North Carolina to visit Janine's store, Memories in the Making.

STICKER TILES

Quick and Easy

Incorporate that great ceramic tile look to your scrapbook pages! Pool side photos are enhanced with stickers mounted onto colored cardstock and then cut into one inch paper tiles.

Above: A few random paper tiles were replaced with photo squares - excess pieces of "water" trimmed from the photographs.

Autumn in Williamsburg

Each Fall we look forward to the changing leaves and the cool autumn air. We enjoy going to Busch Gardens to view all of the beautiful fall flowers and their festive decorations. This year we especially enjoyed the scenery in the new Ireland section. It opened for the first time in the spring - 2001.

LITTLE SISTER

BIG SISTER

Above: Photographs are double mounted on cardstock. The background mat is cut to a 4 square x 5 square size (see Quick Grid Guide page 15.) Foreground mat is cut to make a 1/16 inch border that adds a little boost of color and contrast.

Stickers were mounted on cardstock that was a few shades lighter than background paper and cut into one inch squares before mounting onto grid paper.

Title/Journaling Square is located in the opposite corner from the large sticker tile design to add interest to juxtaposed photographs and lend balance to the page.

Cape Hatteras Lighthouse

Cape Hatteras Lighthouse was built in 1870. The light towered 208 feet in height and was located 1,500 feet from the water's edge. It is the tallest lighthouse in the United States.

Due to erosion problems a campaign was initiated to save the light house from the sea. Sand bags and barrier walls slowed erosion but the sea continues to threaten the historic landmark. A stormy sea in December 1980 brought the tide to a point approximately 50 feet from the lighthouse.

In just a couple of months work will begin to move the lighthouse inland. We decided to make a visit before the location change.

September 1998
National Seashore North Carolina

MOSAIC ANGLES

When several photographs are used to create a mosaic page, the image as a whole becomes greater than the sum of it's parts. A photo mosaic can allow us to see a subject from several angles at the same time or offer us the opportunity to recreate memories of a subject at play.

Photos of buildings, animals, scenery, or inanimate objects might seem dull or uninteresting when they are simply mounted in an album. The use of a grid, brings new

interest to the above scenic lighthouse photos. They seem
to be the perfect subjects for the photo mosaic process.

During the photo mosaic process, capturing the essence of
a National Historic site or scenic treasure becomes a puzzle-
like game. Choosing the photographs, deciding where to
make cuts, which pieces to retain, and which to set aside,
makes each photo mosaic a unique creative experience.

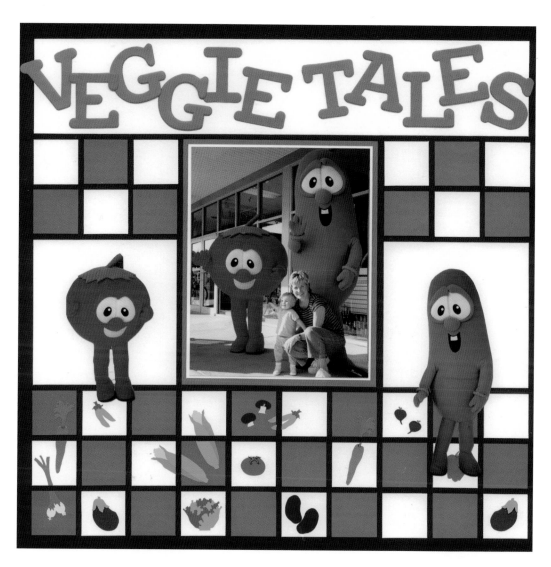

Below: Space Center
By Sandi Keene

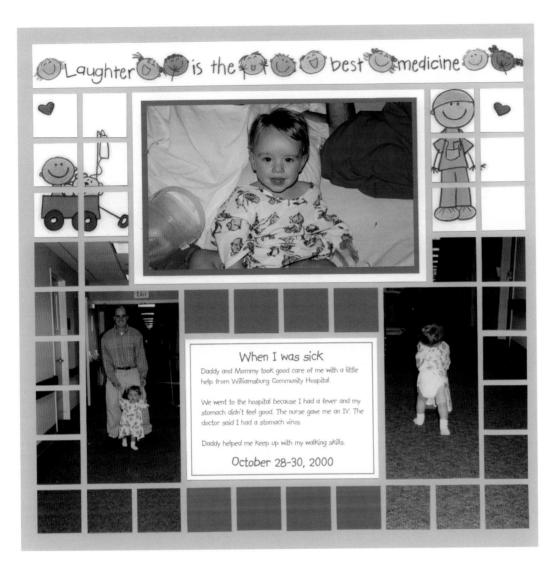

Laughter is the best medicine

When I was sick

Daddy and Mommy took good care of me with a little help from Williamsburg Community Hospital.

We went to the hospital because I had a fever and my stomach didn't feel good. The nurse gave me an IV. The doctor said I had a stomach virus.

Daddy helped me keep up with my walking skills.

October 28-30, 2000

Below: Rocky MTN NP
By Kristen King

ROCKY MTN. N.P.

FALL RIVER PASS
Elev. 11,796
VISITOR CENTER   STORE
INFORMATION · EXHIBITS   GIFTS · LUNCHES

Duck, North Carolina
June 2001
Steve, Anita, and Emmaline

Special Thanks to the following:

Me and My Big Ideas, 30152 Esperanza Pkwy, Rancho Santa Margarita, CA 92688

Mrs. Grossman's Paper Co, P.O. Box 4467, Petaluma, CA 94955

Paper Adventures, Inc., P.O. Box 04393, Milwaukee, WI 53204

Susan Branch published and distributed by Colorbok, P.O. Box 188, Dexter, MI 48130

Printworks, 12342 McCann DR., Santa Fe Springs, CA 90670

Wish in the Wind, 3356 Ironbound Road #103, Williamsburg, VA 23188